The Woolly Prawn

Happy Knitting and crochet.
Best wishes, Jenny

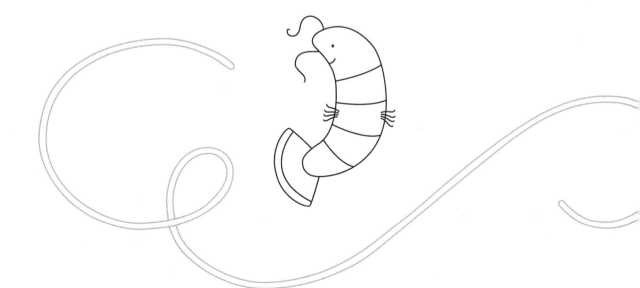

The Woolly Prawn

knit and crochet : any ability : experiment and enjoy

Sian Goulding & Jenny Every

PRAWN PUBLISHING

First published 2012 by Prawn Publishing,
28 Park Lane, Bewdley, Worcestershire,
DY12 2EU, United Kingdom

ISBN: 978-0-9574836-0-6

A catalogue record for this book is available from the
British Library.

Design and illustrations by Katie Walter
Photography by Duncan Woods and Jonathan Goulding

Printed by Bluechilli Design & Print

Contents

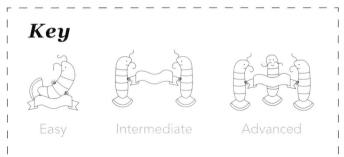

Key

Easy   Intermediate   Advanced

K = Knit   C = Crochet   K & C = Knit & Crochet

The projects

FOR everyone

FOR Pets

FOR LITTLe ones

FOR HER

FOR HIM

FOR SPORT

FOR THE HOME

Welcome

Welcome to the world of The Woolly Prawn. There's nothing quite like a knitted prawn. Whether you are a complete beginner or an accomplished knitter or crocheter I'm pretty certain you won't already have one. So this is your chance, and here are 15 other original and adaptable projects to capture your imagination and get you experimenting with colour, texture and style. You'll also find some snippets of information and inspiration about the wider world of

knitting and crochet – there's some really impressive stuff happening. Be warned though, once you start getting into knitting and crochet, it's a fast road to obsession and you won't want to stop.

Where The Woolly Prawn was born
The inspiration for this book came from a Christmas shopping dash across the internet and around the haberdashery shops. As a thirty something in search

of a creative outlet I recently took up knitting. With an expert mum on hand to show me the basics I quickly became hooked. But when it came to my husband finding an inspiring book with appealing and achievable patterns for me, it just wasn't there.

And so The Woolly Prawn came into being. It's a mum and daughter partnership: a mum with an eye for patterns and a love of colour and experimentation and a daughter who has discovered just how satisfying and fun making things really is.

For me knitting and crochet isn't about dwelling on the intricacies of technique or worrying about tension squares. It's about picking up your needles and hooks, developing your own style, and simply creating. It's about exploring the world of knitting and crochet. There's a whole revolution going on out there, and the revolution really does have something for everyone.

The patterns
There are 16 patterns in this book and all but a couple are short projects which could easily be completed in a weekend. They are graded in terms of difficulty: one prawn is perfect for beginners, two prawn patterns are at a more intermediate level and three prawn patterns are still at an intermediate level but with some more tricky techniques.

You don't find many pattern books which include both knitting and crochet, but combining the two can work really well, particularly when it comes to finishing off projects or adding decorations. The prawns on each pattern tell you whether it is a knit, crochet, or knit and crochet project.

The patterns in this book aren't prescriptive. There is plenty of opportunity for you to add your own individuality or to adapt the patterns in any way you like. You can choose your own yarn, experiment with different size needles and hooks and create your own unique masterpieces. For every pattern the recommended weight of yarn is given. If you want to recreate the pattern and effect exactly, the actual yarns used are listed on page 90.

The techniques
Yes, we go through some of the techniques, but really the best way to learn is to sit next to someone who can knit or crochet and ask them to show you the basics. Or there is a fantastic range of online tutorials which do the same job.

All you need to get started on the patterns in this book is to be able to cast on and off, knit, purl, increase and decrease. Where any additional techniques are needed they are included alongside the relevant pattern. For crochet, as long as you can make a chain, double crochet and work a treble you'll be fine.

Above all I believe knitting and crochet is about having fun, being creative and experimenting. Don't take it too seriously, enjoy it, and discover the parts which inspire you most. Whether your thing is knitting up squares and joining them into an enormous blanket, making presents for friends and family, or going on late night guerrilla knitting installation missions, I hope there's something in this book for you.

Sian Goulding

The tools

You don't need fancy tools to get started with the projects in this book. Once you've got needles and a hook then you're away. But which needles and hooks to choose?

Needles come in a huge range of sizes and materials. Until fairly recently aluminium needles were the most widely available, but now there are colourful and lightweight plastic needles, wooden needles – bamboo and exotic hardwoods, and my personal favourite, birch. Birch needles are a bit pricier but are perfect for beginners because they are light and smooth, but not so slippery that the stitches slide off the end.

Needles come in different lengths and sizes. Shorter length needles are easier to manoeuvre but have less space for stitches. You also get needles of different diameter, from really fine 2mm to very chunky 20mm. In general, the finer the yarn you are using, the thinner the needle you use. Chunky needles make open, big stitches and fine needles produce a tighter weave with little stitches. There is lots of scope to experiment with needle size and yarn to find the effects that you like best.

In the UK needles are labelled with their metric size, but older needles have a number printed on them that doesn't relate to the metric size, and American needles have a different system altogether. Here's a conversion chart to help.

Conversion chart

UK	Metric	US
14	2mm	0
13	2.25mm	1
12	2.75mm	2
11	3mm	-
10	3.25mm	3
-	3.5mm	4
9	3.75mm	5
8	4mm	6
7	4.5mm	7
6	5mm	8
5	5.5mm	9
4	6mm	10
3	6.5mm	10.5
2	7mm	-
1	7.5mm	-
0	8mm	11
00	9mm	13

Crochet hooks come in different sizes and materials too. As with needles, it really is down to personal choice. For most projects in this book you will need a 4mm hook – the most common size for double knitting projects. You can get different effects with different combinations of hook size and type of yarn. Using a thick hook with a fine yarn will produce a more lacy effect and using a thinner hook with any yarn will make a more dense fabric with less stretch – perfect for cushion covers and bags but not so good for clothes.

Other useful accessories are scissors, a tapestry needle (a larger version of a sewing needle with a big eye and a blunt end) for seaming and sewing in ends, a tape measure, pins for when you are stitching up and a row counter so you can keep track of the rows you have knitted.

There are masses of online options for accessories, yarns, patterns and forums. Here are a few tried and tested favourites:

Purplelinda Crafts **www.purplelindacrafts.co.uk**: specialists in crochet supplies.

Get Knitted **www.getknitted.com**: an online version of the popular Bristol shop.

McA direct **www.mcadirect.com**: all kinds of knitting accessories at good prices.

Modern Knitting **www.modernknitting.co.uk**: a big online store with a great choice of yarns.

Ravelry **www.ravelry.com**: like Facebook for knitters and crocheters.

Etsy **www.etsy.com**: a vibrant craft marketplace where you can buy and sell handmade or vintage items and supplies.

YouTube **www.youtube.com**: great for tutorials.

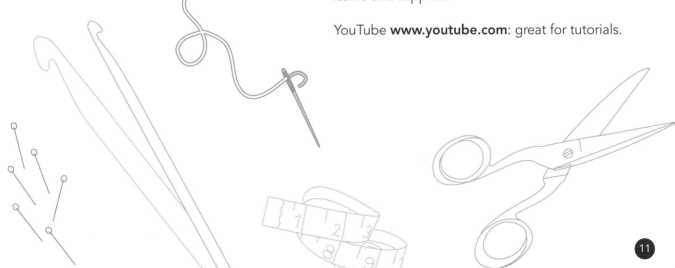

The yarn

Let's talk about yarn. Yarn might sound like an old fashioned word, but it is the best word to use. Wool really refers only to 100% wool, so yarn includes all the other blends and materials too.

Experimenting with different yarns is one of the best bits about knitting and crochet but choosing your yarn can be confusing as there are so many different types out there. The thickness of the yarn you choose determines the thickness of the fabric produced – chunkier yarn combined with thicker needles makes for a fast growing piece of work.

> **The thickness of the yarn is referred to as the weight. These are the weights you are most likely to come across:**
>
> - 2 and 3ply – lace weight
> - 4ply – most sock wool is 4ply
> - Double knit – most commonly used, medium weight, often used with 4mm needles and hooks
> - Aran
> - Chunky – good for cold weather outer wear
> - Super chunky – super good for cold weather outer wear

Yarn is usually sold in balls of 50g or 100g, but it is also important to look on the label for the length of yarn in the ball. Once you know this you can work out how much yarn is needed for a particular pattern and then you can substitute the recommended yarn with your own choice.

For crochet, it's pretty much the same. You can crochet with the same yarns as you knit with, although you also find specific crochet cottons which are good for fine lacework.

What is your yarn?
Nowadays an impressive array of materials can be spun into yarn ranging from the completely natural 100% wool, cotton, bamboo, mohair, alpaca, cashmere and silk to the completely man-made such as acrylic, polyamide and nylon. And there are lots of blends that combine both. Knitting or crocheting with a natural yarn gives a different feel and effect from doing the same pattern with a man-made yarn.

Pricewise, man-made yarns tend to be cheapest starting from around £1.50 for 50g while silk and cashmere are among the most expensive at around £10 for 50g. There are some great brands of budget yarns available like King Cole, Sirdar and Stylecraft which offer a wide selection of man-made and natural yarns, or more upmarket ranges from the likes of Debbie Bliss, Rowan and Jillybeans. Choosing your yarn is one of the many pleasures of knitting and crochet. Go to a knitting shop to get an idea of what the yarn feels like, check the texture and the colour, even if you then opt to buy online.

Whether you choose a natural or man-made yarn can depend on your budget, the finished effect you want, whether the item will be worn next to skin (some people don't like wearing wool next to their skin) and whether the item will need to be washed frequently. Many natural yarns need to be hand washed (so they don't shrink) although some wool is treated so it can be machine washed. Man-made yarns are much easier to wash as you can simply throw them in the machine. Just check the washing instructions on the yarn label.

For the patterns in this book we recommend the weight of yarn to use but we don't specify a particular brand or yarn content. It's about you deciding on the look, colour and feel that you want. Try out some different textures. Using a mixture of yarns for projects will make your results more interesting, colourful and unique.

Tension squares

Many patterns mention tension squares – making a 10cm square with your yarn so you get an idea of how it knits up. It can be a good idea if you are substituting a yarn and especially if you are making clothes, but for most of the projects in this book, tension isn't vital. Where the size of the item is important tension is mentioned in the pattern.

Colour

A huge part of the fun of knitting and crochet is being able to use and experiment with different colours. In the 1970s Kaffe Fassett, referred to as the 'master of colour and pattern design', inspired many with his bold and creative approach to colour. Using a photo or painting as inspiration for colour choices he encouraged knitters to take free reign and explore colour work not being afraid of introducing maybe 50 colours into one piece.

Nowadays you don't just get single colour balls of yarn, you can buy self-patterning (or striping) yarns and hand painted yarns, which are produced in brilliant colours and produce great effects. This is by far the easiest way to incorporate different shades and colours into your work.

Using different coloured yarns to knit or crochet in stripes is another way to achieve good colour effects. Stripes are most often worked in stocking stitch over an even number of rows so that the colour change always takes place at the beginning of a knit row and the yarn or yarns not in use can then be carried up the side of your work until next required (as in the mix and match blanket).

Slip stitch or mosaic knitting is a clever technique for producing colour effects. It creates complex stitch patterns and textures but you only ever use one colour per row (as in the tea cosy and child's scarf).

More complicated is 'intarsia' which is adding motifs or pictures using small bobbins with the different colours at the back of your work. Fair Isle is the most complex of all, where the colour is incorporated through symmetrical patterns. Neither of these are needed for the patterns in this book, but you can find plenty of advice and tutorials on them online.

Abbreviations

These are the knitting and crochet abbreviations used in this book.

Knitting

K	knit
P	purl
st(s)	stitch(es)
st st	stocking stitch (knit one row, purl one row)
beg	beginning
dec	decrease
k2tog	knit the next two stitches together
p2tog	purl the next two stitches together
psso	pass slipped stitch over stitch just knitted
k2togtbl	knit the next two stitches together through the back loops
inc	increase
kfb	knit into the front and back of next stitch
m1	make one stitch – by picking up the horizontal loop lying before the next stitch and knitting into the back of it
sl1	slip one – slip next stitch onto the right-hand needle without knitting it
kw	knitwise (as if to knit it but don't)
pw	purlwise (as if to purl it but don't)
sk2po	slip one, knit two together, pass slipped stitch over thus decreasing by two stitches

rs	right side (front of work)
ws	wrong side (back of work)
rep	repeat
rem	remaining
yf	bring yarn to front of work
yb	take yarn to back of work
yo	bring yarn to front between points of needles and take back over the right needle to knit the next stitch
alt	alternate

Crochet

Crochet patterns use many of the same abbreviations as knitting. Here are the crochet specific ones you will come across in this book.

ch	chain
sp(s)	space(s)
lp(s)	loop(s)
yo	yarn over hook
sl st	slip stitch
dc	double crochet
tr	treble
htr	half treble
dtr	double treble
sk	skip
rnd	round

Casting on

There are several ways of casting on and they all begin with a slip knot. The method used for the projects in this book is known as cable casting on and is done with two needles.

1. Create a slip knot by making a loop at the end of the yarn and use one of your needles to pull up a second loop through the first one. Tighten the knot on the needle and you have your first stitch.

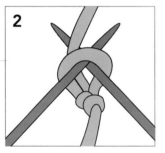

2. Holding the needle with the slip knot in your left hand insert the point of the other needle up into the slip knot. With the ball end of the yarn in your right hand wrap it anticlockwise round the tip of the right needle.

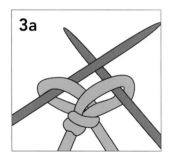

3a. Draw the loop of yarn through to the front until it is loose enough to transfer to the left needle.

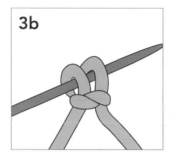

3b. You now have two stitches on this needle. Insert the right needle between the two stitches on the left needle from front to back.

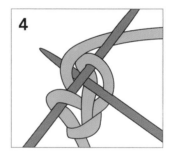

4. Wrap the yarn anticlockwise round the tip of the right needle.

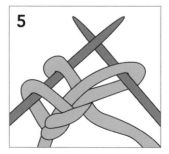

5. Draw the yarn through the gap between the stitches to make a loop large enough to transfer onto the left needle – three stitches have now been cast on.

Repeat steps 4 and 5 until you have as many stitches on your needle as you need.

The stitches

All knitting patterns are worked in either knit or purl stitches. When you knit on straight needles you work across all the stitches on one row transferring them from the left to the right needle as you work them. Then you turn the needles around to begin the next row so that the needle with the stitches is in your left hand again.

The knit stitch

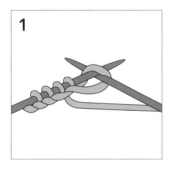

1. Hold the needle with the cast-on stitches in your left hand. Keep the yarn at the back of this needle. Insert the point of the other needle from front to back into the front loop of the first stitch.

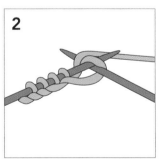

3. Pull the yarn through the stitch to form a loop on your right needle.

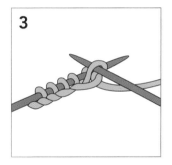

2. Holding the yarn in your right hand wrap it round the right needle tip anticlockwise from back to front.

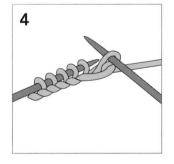

4. Slip the original stitch off the left needle by moving your right needle gently to the right. The new stitch will be on the right needle.

Repeat steps 1-4 until all the stitches have been knitted onto the right needle. Transfer the needle to your left hand ready to knit the next row. Knitting every row is called garter stitch and both sides of the knitting look the same.

The purl stitch

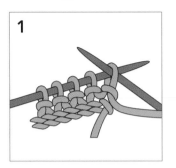

1. Hold the needle with the stitches in your left hand with the yarn at the front of the work. Insert the right needle into the front loop of the first stitch from right to left, back to front.

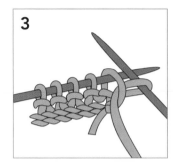

2. Wrap the yarn round the right needle tip taking it anticlockwise from right to left.

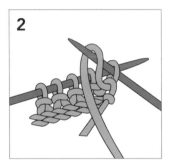

3. Pull the yarn back through the stitch to form a loop on the right needle – your purl stitch.

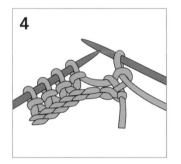

4. Move your right needle away gently so that the original stitch slips off the left needle and your new stitch is on the right needle.

Repeat steps 1-4 until all the stitches have been purled onto the right needle. When you transfer this needle to your left hand again the right side of your work will be facing you and you will be ready to knit across the next row. Alternate rows of knit and purl stitches create stocking stitch, a smoother fabric than garter stitch. The knit rows are on the right side of the work and the purl rows are on the wrong side.

Casting off

When each piece of knitting is finished the last row of stitches need to be secured so that the work does not unravel. This is called casting off.

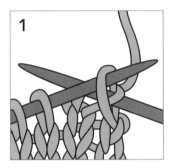

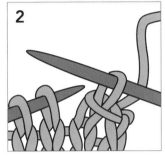

1. Knit the first two stitches onto the right needle. With the tip of the left needle lift the first stitch you knitted over the second one and off the right needle – one stitch left.

2. Knit the next stitch from the left needle so that you have two stitches on the right needle again. Lift the first stitch over the second as in step 1.

Repeat steps 1 and 2 until all the stitches from the left needle have been knitted onto the right needle and cast off and you have one stitch left on the right needle. Cut the yarn leaving a 10cm tail, thread this through the last stitch and pull gently to tighten.

If the pattern asks you to cast off purlwise you follow steps 1 and 2 in the same way but purl the stitches instead of knitting them.

Yarn ends need to be woven into the seams or along a row of stitches at the back of the work using a blunt tapestry needle with a large eye.

Shaping

The fabric which you are creating can be shaped by increasing or decreasing the number of stitches on your needle. The following are the most frequently used ways of doing this.

To increase

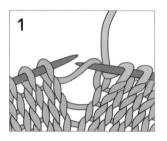

Make 1 (m1)

1. Using the tip of your right needle lift the horizontal bar between the stitch you have just worked and the next one and transfer it onto the left needle.

2+3. Knit into the back of the loop created and slip the new stitch off the left needle onto the right needle.

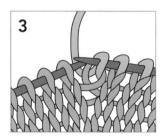

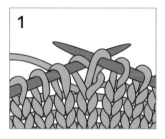

Knit into front and back (kfb)

1. Knit into the front loop of the stitch as normal but don't slip the stitch off the left needle.

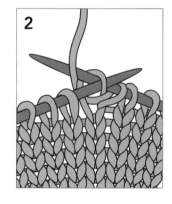

2. Now insert the right needle into the back loop of the same stitch. Take the yarn round the needle and pull it through to make a second stitch. Slip the original stitch off the left needle – you have replaced it with two new stitches on your right needle.

To decrease

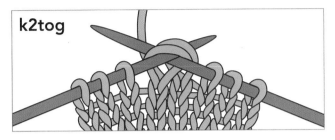

k2tog

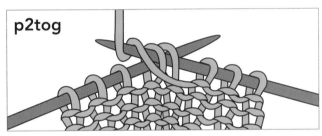

p2tog

The easiest way to decrease is by knitting or purling two stitches together, working them as if they are one stitch. The abbreviations for these decreases are k2tog and p2tog and the stitches produced slope to the right.

Sometimes a decrease stitch which slopes to the left may be needed and then the technique will be different. It may be written as k2togtbl – knit two together through the back loop or sl1k1psso – slip one, knit one, pass slipped stitch over.

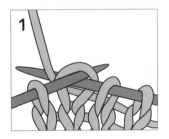

sl1k1psso

1. Insert the right needle into the front loop of the next stitch as if to knit it but simply slip it off the left needle onto the right one – this is also known as slip one knitwise. Knit the next stitch as normal.

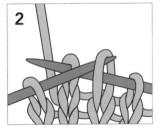

2. With the tip of the left needle lift the slipped stitch up and over the last knitted stitch and off the right needle.

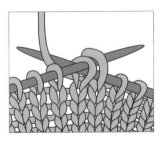

k2togtbl

Insert the right needle into the back loops of the next two stitches and knit together as if they were one.

Other techniques

Picking up stitches

Sometimes you need to create new stitches along the edge of a finished piece of knitting, either horizontally along a cast-on or cast-off edge or vertically along a side edge.

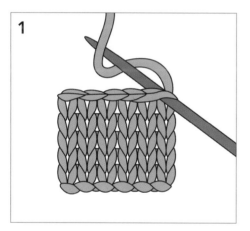

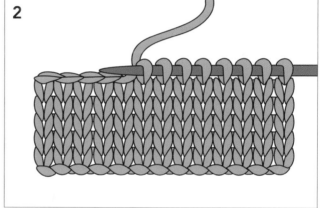

Horizontal pick up

1. Hold the needle in your right hand and have the right side of the work facing you. From front to back insert the needle point into the centre of the first stitch under both loops. Wrap the yarn round the needle as if to knit.

2. Draw the loop through to the front – one stitch picked up. Continue to pick up along the edge in this way until you have the number of stitches you need, spacing them out evenly if the number of pick-up stitches is more or less than the number of stitches along the edge.

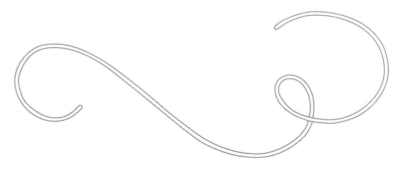

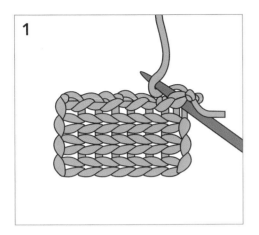

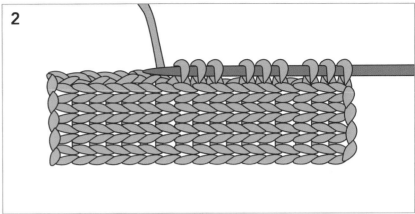

Vertical pick up

1. With right side of work facing insert the needle point into the edge stitch of the first row under both loops. Wrap the yarn round the needle as if to knit.

2. Draw the loop through and continue to pick up in this way along the edge until you have the number of stitches you need.

When you pick up stitches along the side of a piece of knitting the row ends will be your guide. There are often more rows than stitches required so you will need to space your pick-up stitches evenly along the edge by measuring your edge and dividing it up into sections.

Joining in a new ball of yarn or a different colour

Whether you need to join in your next ball of yarn or another colour it is always best to do this at the beginning of a row. Leave a 15cm tail of both the old and the new yarn – you can loosely tie the tail of new yarn around the other one if you wish (this knot should be opened when the work is finished and the tails woven into the seam). Drop the old yarn and work the first stitch of the row with your new yarn or colour. If you are working narrow stripes in two or three colours the yarns which you are not using can be carried up the side of the work rather than cut at the end of each stripe.

Putting it all together

There are lots of ways of joining pieces of knitting and everybody has their own preference. Whichever method you choose you need a tapestry needle and a length of the yarn with which the item has been made unless it is very chunky and then it is best to find a thinner, matching thread.

Mattress stitch

This method produces a neat, invisible seam and can be used on vertical or horizontal edges. It is always worked from right to left with the right sides of your knitting facing you. This helps you to see exactly how the seam is progressing and accurately match stripes or patterns as you go.

Vertical (rows to rows)

1. Lay your two pieces of knitting edge to edge right sides up. From the front take your needle down between the edge stitch and the second stitch of the first row of one piece. Now take the needle under the next row and bring up through to the front again pulling the yarn through and leave a 10cm tail of yarn.

2. Take the needle to the other piece of work, insert into the space between the edge stitch and second stitch of the first row. Pass the needle under the loops of two rows before bringing it back up to the front.

3. Take the needle back to the space where the yarn came up on the first edge, insert it and pass it under the loops of the next two rows before coming back up.

Continue to work from edge to edge in this way, gently pulling your yarn to close the seam after every few stitches. Leaving a loose tail at the beginning means you can rework part of your seam if stripes do not match exactly or it is not a perfect fit. When the seam is done weave the yarn ends into the work to secure them.

Horizontal (stitches to stitches)

1. Lay your two pieces edge to edge with right sides up. From the back of the work bring your needle up through the centre of the corner stitch of one piece leaving a 10cm tail of yarn.

2. Take the needle over to the other piece and from the back of the work bring it up between the first and second stitches.

3. Take the needle back to the first piece and insert it into the space where the yarn came up. Pass it under two loops and bring it back up to the front.

Continue to work from side to side along the edge matching the stitches as you go and easing the seam closed gently after every few stitches. When complete fasten off both ends securely into the seam.

Oversewing

This produces a flat seam which is particularly good for sewing up small items and for baby clothes where a ridge in the fabric could be uncomfortable.

Pin or hold the two pieces in place with right sides together and secure your yarn at one end. Take your yarn from front to back over the edge of the seam and out through the front again catching the loops at the very edge of each piece and moving along a couple of stitches each time.

Back stitch

This method produces a strong seam and works better with lightweight yarns because the seam tends to be more bulky. For this reason it is important to keep your stitches as near to the edge of the work as you can.

1. Pin the pieces of knitting in place with right sides together so the wrong side of the work is facing you. Bring your needle up through the knitting at the right-hand end, one stitch or row from the edge. Take the needle round the two edges to secure them and bring it back up through the double thickness of knitting, one stitch further along the edge to be joined.

2. Insert the needle into the work at the point where the first stitch began and bring it back up two stitches further along to the left.

Continue to sew up the seam in this way working one stitch back at the front and two stitches forward at the back. Take care not to pull the yarn too tightly after each stitch.

Crochet - the basics

In crochet there is only ever one stitch being worked at any time so you don't need to worry about casting on or off or dropped stitches. Crochet stitches are always worked into a base which can be a length of foundation chain or a ring made from chains. Each stitch is quite simply a loop of yarn drawn through another loop.

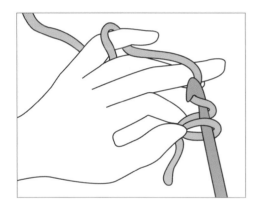

Holding the hook and yarn

There is no right or wrong way to hold the crochet hook and yarn. The best way is the one which feels most comfortable to you and the ideal way to get the hang of it is to get someone to show you. Online tutorials like the ones on Ravelry and YouTube can also be very helpful. Traditionally the hook is held like a pen in the right hand and the yarn is held and controlled with the left hand.

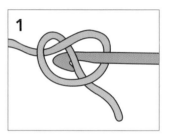

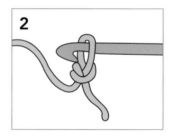

Making a slip knot

Make a loop in the yarn, insert the hook and catch the strand of yarn at the back. Pull the loop through and gently tighten both ends of yarn to close the loop on the hook.

The stitches

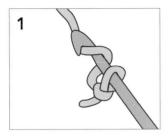

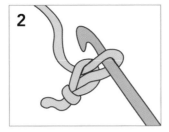

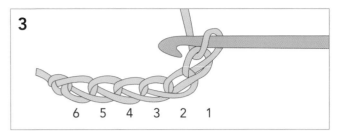

Chain (ch)

Almost all crochet projects begin with a length of chain stitches called a foundation chain, and chains often appear within patterns as well. A chain is always worked in the same way.

With the slip knot or active stitch on your hook and the working yarn in your left hand dip the tip of the hook under the yarn from front to back. Catch the yarn and draw it through the slip knot or active stitch allowing the

slip knot or stitch to slip off the hook. Keep the chain stitch which you have made fairly loose as you will be working into it in your first row. Continue to make the number of chains you need in this way.

If you are following a pattern, it is important to count the chains carefully – the loop on the hook does not count as a stitch but the slip knot does.

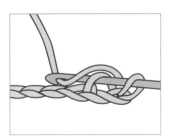

Slip stitch (sl st)

This stitch does not add height to your work. It is used for moving across stitches or joining. Insert the hook into the chain or indicated stitch, catch the yarn and draw it through both that stitch and the loop on your hook in one movement.

Stitch height

All the stitches used in crochet are worked in a similar way to making a chain, by catching the yarn with your hook and drawing it through. The height of the stitch depends on the number of times you wrap the yarn round the hook before inserting it into a stitch and drawing the loop through. When working into a stitch the hook should be inserted from front to

back under the top two threads of the stitch unless the pattern specifies working only into the front or back loop (fl or bl) as in the cushion cover (p86). At the beginning of a row you will often be asked to make turning chain to bring your work up to the height of the stitch which you are using. This is usually one chain for double crochet, two chain for half trebles and three chain for trebles.

Double crochet (dc)
There are two steps to this stitch.

1. Insert the hook into the chain or stitch indicated, wrap the yarn round the hook and draw it through the chain or stitch only – two loops on hook.

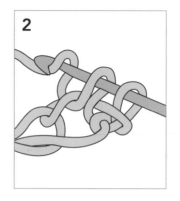

2. Wrap the yarn round the hook again and pull it through both the loops on the hook – one loop left and one double crochet made.

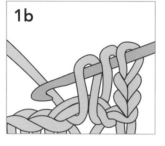

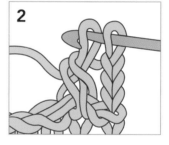

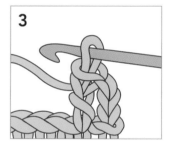

Treble crochet (tr)
At the beginning of a row of trebles you may be asked to work two or three chain stitches and these usually count as the first stitch of the row. There are three steps to this stitch.

1a. Wrap the yarn round the hook by dipping the tip of the hook under the yarn from front to back.

1b. Now insert the hook into the stitch indicated and catch the yarn round the hook again. Draw the loop through – three loops on hook.

2. Wrap the yarn round the hook again and draw this new loop through the first two loops already on the hook slipping them off as you do so – two loops left.

3. Wrap the yarn round the hook again and draw the loop through the remaining two loops on the hook – one loop left and one treble crochet made.

Half treble (htr)

Between a double and treble crochet in height, this stitch is worked exactly like a treble to the end of step 1. Then wrap the yarn round the hook again and pull through all three loops at the same time – one loop left, one half treble made.

Double treble (dtr) and triple treble (trtr)

Variations on trebles, these are worked in the same way but with extra wraps round the hook before inserting it into the work. Wrap twice for a double treble and three times for a triple treble. Each extra wrap will give one extra step and extra height at the end as you loop the yarn round the hook and bring it through two loops at a time until only one is left on your hook.

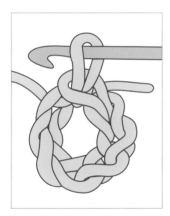

Working in rounds

Sometimes crochet is worked in a circle, for example to begin a granny square or to create a round shape. This means you start off by making a chain circle into which you work your first round of double or treble crochet stitches. Crochet the number of chains required on the pattern and join them into a circle with a slip stitch. Do this by inserting the hook into the first chain made (not the slip knot), then wrap the yarn round the hook, pull it through the chain and the loop on the hook at the same time.

Joining in a new yarn or colour

When you are working in stripes or changing colour in the middle of a row the best way to join in a new yarn is on the stitch before the colour change. In the case of stripes this will be the last stitch of the previous row or round. When you reach this stitch work the old yarn until the last two loops of the stitch remain. Drop the old yarn at the back of the work and wrap the new yarn round the hook to complete the stitch – the loop on your hook will now be in the new colour and the loose ends can be woven into the back of the work.

When making a granny square you may need to join your new colour into a space rather than a stitch. To do this you make a slip knot on your hook in the new colour, insert the hook into the space indicated, wrap the yarn over the hook and pull it through both the space and the slip knot. This secures the new yarn in place.

Knitting as art

Guerrilla knitting, graffiti knitting, urban knitting, yarnbombing and yarnstorming – they sound pretty current and exciting, and they are. They are all about the same thing – showcasing knitting, livening up public spaces, revealing the fun side of knitting and bringing a smile to people's faces.

Magda Sayeg, a clothes shop owner from Texas started the craze. She wanted to liven up all the glass, concrete and steel around her with something handmade. In 2005 Sayeg founded Knitta Please, a knit graffiti group, and since then they have been yarnbombing all over the world including Brooklyn Bridge and covering a bus in Mexico City.

Back in the UK, Knit the City, 'your friendly neighbourhood graffiti knitters' have been yarnstorming across London since 2009. They started with small installations on the South Bank and up-scaled to covering barriers in Covent Garden, installing a telephone box cosy in Parliament Square and a giant squid at the Natural History Museum.

And it's not just happening in London. Project ArtYarn devised by two artists and knitters in Manchester is about making art – their knitting – accessible to all and using the cityscape as a free gallery. In Bristol, Knitiffi, the local collective of knit artists, covered a 20ft boat from bow to stern in colourful knitting. They aim to 'make our world a brighter, happier place' through installations, exhibitions and other covert missions.

You can find books, websites and blogs dedicated to the craze of guerrilla knitting. There is a whole global community out there making public spaces a little bit prettier and more fun. Guerrilla knitting is an art in itself. Don't be too serious or let others take you too seriously. Remember, there are no rules. Go on, have a go, you know you want to...

www.knittaplease.com
www.knitthecity.com
www.artyarn.blogspot.co.uk
http://knitiffi.blogspot.co.uk

FOR
EVERYONE

The Woolly Prawn

Everyone needs a woolly prawn. They are soft, friendly, mischievous little things who love to explore new places and end the day cuddling up somewhere warm with their human companions. You don't see many prawns out and about; there really should be more of them. You could have a whole prawn family in various sizes and shades.

Measurements
Approx 25cm (10in) long

You will need
- Yarn: 1 x 50g (100m) pink aran weight
- Needles: 4.5mm
- Crochet hook: 4mm
- Small amount of toy stuffing
- Small amount of black yarn or buttons for eyes

The body

Cast on 8sts – this will be the tail end.

* Rows 1-3: Knit.
* Row 4: Purl.
* Row 5: (rs) K2, m1, K to last 2sts, m1, K2. [10sts]
* Rows 6 and all even numbered rows except rows 10, 18, 26, 36, 46 and 54: Purl.
* Rows 7+9: as row 5. [14sts]
* Row 10: Knit.
* Row 11: K2, m1, K5, m1, K5, m1, K2. [17sts]
* Rows 12, 13+14: St st beg with purl row.
* Row 15: K2, m1, K6, m1, K7, m1, K2. [20sts]
* Rows 17+18: Knit.
* Row 19: K2, m1, K8, m1, K8, m1, K2. [23sts]
* Row 21: K2, m1, K10, m1, K9, m1, K2. [26sts]
* Row 23: K2, m1, K11, m1, K11, m1, K2. [29sts]
* Row 25+26: Knit.
* Rows 27-30: St st beg with knit row.
* Row 31: K14, turn and purl to end (row 32).
* Row 33: K15, turn and purl to end (row 34).
* Row 35: K16, turn and knit to end (row 36).
* Row 37: K17, turn and purl to end (row 38).
* Rows 39-44: St st beg with knit row.
* Row 45: K2tog, K to last 2sts, k2tog. [27sts]
* Row 46: Knit.
* Row 47: K2tog, K11, k2tog, K10, k2tog. [24sts]
* Rows 48-50: St st beg with purl row.
* Row 51: K2tog, K9, k2tog, K9, k2tog. [21sts]
* Row 53: K2tog, K to last 2sts, k2tog. [19sts]
* Row 54: Knit.
* Rows 55, 57, 59+61: Continue to dec at each end of these rows as in row 53. [11sts]
* Row 62: Cast off.
  Fasten off and weave in loose ends.

To make up

Fold in half lengthwise with right sides together. Backstitch around the head (cast-off) end then leaving the tail end open sew up the seam from each end leaving an opening at the centre large enough to add the stuffing. Turn right side out, stuff the prawn, stitch up remaining side seam and fasten off.

Crochet the tail

Hold the prawn with the right side towards you and with your crochet hook join yarn with a sl st to right hand top corner. Working through the double fabric (where the 8 cast-on sts have been folded together) make 2ch (counts as first htr) then work 1tr into same space as sl st, 2tr across top of tail and (1tr, 1htr) into last stitch (6sts made). Turn. You are now working back along underside of tail. 2ch (counts as first htr), 2tr into same st, 2tr into each of next 4sts, (2tr, 1htr) into last st [14sts]. Fasten off and weave in ends.

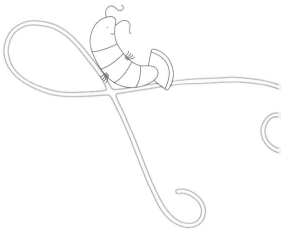

To finish off

Make 2 i-cords (see page 85) each 9cm long and stitch to each side of the head as in the photo. For legs make 10 strips each of 10 foundation chain and attach 5 to the centre of each side of body. Embroider eyes on either side of the head with black yarn or use black buttons.

Bunting

Celebrate with some bunting. Knitted entirely in garter stitch this is an ideal project for new knitters. Choose your colours to reflect the event you are decorating for: match the colour scheme in the nursery, go patriotic with red, white and blue or simply try this pattern in a mixture of different shades to use up some of your yarn stash.

You will need
- Yarn: 4 or 5 x 50g (110m) DK in a variety of colours or oddments from your yarn stash
- Needles: 4mm
- Crochet hook: 4mm (optional, for joining up triangles)

Special note
In this pattern a variation of m1 is used to denote an increase from row 7 onwards instead of kfb. m1 – insert tip of right hand needle purlwise into loop below next stitch, lift this loop onto left hand needle and knit into back of it – one stitch made.

For each triangle
Cast on 1 stitch with a slip knot.
- Row 1: Knit front and back of stitch (kfb). [2sts]
- Row 2: Kfb, K1. [3sts]
- Row 3: K3.
- Row 4: Kfb, kfb, K1. [5sts]
- Rows 5+6: Sl1, K4.
- Row 7: Sl1, m1 (see note), K to last 2sts, m1, K1. [7sts]
- Rows 8+9: Sl1, K6.
- Row 10: Sl1, m1, K to last 2sts, m1, K1. [9sts]
- Rows 11+12: Sl1, K8.
  Continue to increase 2sts as in rows 7+10 on next and every following 3rd row until you have 27sts on needle (37 rows worked).
- Row 38: Sl1, knit to end.
  Cast off. Fasten off and weave in ends at tops of triangles. Make as many triangles as you need.

To make up
Either stitch the tops of the triangles onto a length of ribbon, an i-cord (see page 85) or you can crochet them together as follows:

Make 80 foundation chain with the crochet hook and colour of your choice. Sl st into each of the 27 cast-off stitches across top of triangle, *12ch and work across the top of next triangle in the same way. Rep from * until you have joined all the triangles, work another 80ch and turn.

Next row: 2ch, 1dc into next st and every st to end.

Fasten off. Using the yarn end left at point of each triangle sew on a small bell.

Mix & match blanket

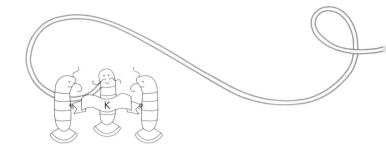

This is a great project for experimenting with new stitch patterns and textures. You can create your own masterpiece and have some fun designing your own colour scheme.

Measurements
Approx 75cm x 55cm (30in x 22in)

You will need
• Yarn: 12 x 50g (115m) DK in an assortment of colours
• Needles: 4mm
• 3.25mm circular needle for the edging

Stitch patterns
This blanket is made up of textured squares combined with stocking stitch striped squares. Each square should be worked until it measures 10cm (4in) ending on the wrong side. For the striped squares cast on 24sts and work in stocking stitch. The multiples are included in case you want to adapt these stitch patterns for larger projects.

The pattern is based on 5 strips of 7 squares each measuring 10cm by 10cm (4in x 4in) but instead of having 35 individual squares to join together, you make this blanket in strips. Pick up the required number of stitches along the right side of the cast-off edge of the first square of each strip instead of casting on a new square – this then counts as row 1 of the pattern for the next square. The 5 strips are joined together with mattress stitch and you can add as many strips as you like to make a blanket of any size.

Any DK yarn can be used for this project but bear in mind that the blanket may need washing so a machine washable yarn might be best.

This isn't a prescriptive pattern; it really is a case of making up the blanket to any design you want. You just need to remember that any variations of rib (K1, P1) tend to produce a narrower fabric than other combinations of knit and purl stitches, so you would need to cast on more stitches to make a 10cm (4in) square. Striped squares are worked in stocking stitch in any colour combinations and the width of the stripes can be varied as you wish.

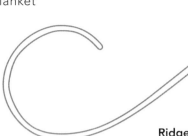

Moss stitch (multiple of 2+1)

Cast on 23sts.

- Row 1: K1, *P1, K1; rep from * to end of row.
  Every row is the same and right and wrong sides of work look the same; continue until work measures 10cm (4in). Cast off in pattern.

Double moss stitch (multiple of 2+1, a 4 row pattern)

Cast on 23sts.

- Row 1: (rs) K1, *P1, K1; rep from * to end.
- Row 2: (ws) P1, *K1, P1; rep from * to end.
- Row 3: As row 2.
- Row 4: As row 1.

Box stitch (multiple of 4+2, a 4 row pattern)

Cast on 22sts.

- Row 1: (rs) K2, *P2, K2; rep from * to end.
- Row 2: (ws) P2, *K2, P2; rep from * to end.
- Row 3: As row 2.
- Row 4: As row 1.

Rice stitch (multiple of 2, a 2 row pattern)

Cast on 24sts.

- Row 1: *K1, P1; rep from * to end.
- Row 2: Knit to end.

Ridged rib (multiple of 2+1, a 4 row pattern)

Cast on 23sts.

- Row 1: (rs) Knit.
- Row 2: (ws) Knit.
- Row 3: P1, *K1, P1; rep from * to end.
- Row 4: K1, *P1, K1; rep from * to end.

Interrupted rib (multiple of 2+1, a 4 row pattern)

Cast on 23sts.

- Row 1: (rs) P1, *K1, P1; rep from * to end.
- Row 2: (ws) K1, *P1, K1; rep from * to end.
- Row 3: Purl.
- Row 4: Knit.

Basket weave (multiple of 4+3, a 4 row pattern)

Cast on 23sts.

- Row 1: (rs) Knit.
- Row 2: (ws) *K3, P1; rep from * to last 3sts, K3.
- Row 3: Knit.
- Row 4: K1, *P1, K3; rep from * to last 2sts, P1, K1.

Woven stitch (multiple of 2+1, a 4 row pattern)

Cast on 23sts.

- Row 1: (rs) K1, *yf, sl1, yb, K1; rep from * to end.
- Row 2: (ws) Purl.
- Row 3: K2, *yf, sl1, yb, K1; rep from * to last st, K1.
- Row 4: Purl.

To make up

When you have completed 5 strips of 7 squares and woven in any loose ends block and press the strips according to instructions on the ball bands. Join the 5 strips using mattress stitch.

Edging

Using 3.25mm circular needle and one of your 3 chosen edging colours (or if you prefer, just use one colour) and with right side of work facing pick up and knit 25sts per square up right side of blanket. [175sts]

- Row 1: (ws) Kfb into first st, K to last 2sts, kfb into next st, K1.
- Row 2: Knit.
- Row 3: Kfb into first st, K to last 2sts, kfb into next st, K1.
- Row 4: Join in 2nd colour, knit to end.
- Row 5: In 2nd colour, kfb into first st, K to last 2sts, kfb into next st, K1.
- Row 6: Join in 3rd colour, kfb into first st, K to last 2sts, kfb into next st, K1.
- Row 7: In 3rd colour knit.
- Row 8: Cast off in 3rd colour.

Work edging for the left side in the same way. Repeat this 8 row edging for the top and bottom of blanket in the same colours but picking up one stitch from each stitch along the cast-on and cast-off edges. Join the slanted edges at each corner by oversewing at back of work.

Hyperbolic crochet

Hyperbolic crochet was discovered in 1997 by Cornell University mathematician Dr. Daina Taimina. She used crochet to make a tactile version of the hyperbolic plane and other hyperbolic surfaces. Taimina made models that vividly illustrated these geometrically problematic shapes.

Now for a bit of geometry, and this is pretty phenomenal stuff. The hyperbolic plane is the geometric opposite of a sphere. On a sphere, the surface curves in on itself and is closed. A hyperbolic plane is a surface where the space curves away from itself at every point. Until Taimina's models, mathematicians believed it was impossible to construct physical models of hyperbolic forms, yet nature had been doing just that for hundreds of millions of years.

At first Taimina had tried knitting, and you can knit hyperbolic surfaces, but the large number of stitches on the needles quickly becomes unmanageable. Soon Taimina realised that crochet offered the better approach. To crochet a hyperbolic structure you simply increase stitches at a regular rate in every row. The more often you increase, the more quickly the model will ruffle up.

Taimina's crochet models have been exhibited by the Institute For Figuring in Los Angeles and her work was the inspiration behind the Hyperbolic Crochet Coral Reef project created in 2005 by Christine and Margaret Wertheim. This project really is a fusion of mathematics, marine biology and community art.

These Australian sisters elaborated on Taimina's techniques to model a whole range of reef-like forms including organisms with hyperbolic properties such as kelps, anemones, sea slugs and corals. What started as a project to raise awareness of the threats of pollution and global warming of the Great Barrier Reef has grown into a global community art project with a touring exhibition and satellite reefs popping up across the world.

www.crochetcoralreef.org

For Little ones

Child's scarf

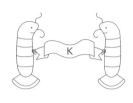

For anyone who loves experimenting with colour this scarf is an ideal way to try out colourwork without the hassle of Fair Isle or intarsia. Only one colour is used on any row but this slip stitch pattern makes the finished effect look much more complex.

Measurements
102cm (40in) long and 3cm (5in) wide

You will need
• Yarn: 1 x 50g (135m) soft chunky yarn in each of 3 colours, A, B and C
• Needles: 5.5mm

Special note
Carry the colours not in use up the side of your work as you go.

Cast on 27sts in yarn A.

- Rows 1+2: Knit.

  Join in yarn B.
- Row 3: K1,*sl1pw, K1; rep from * to end.
- Row 4: K1, *yf, sl1, yb, K1; rep from * to end.

  Join in yarn C.
- Rows 5+6: Knit.

  Change to yarn A.
- Row 7: K2, *sl1pw, K1; rep from * to last 2 sts, K2.
- Row 8: K2, *yf, sl1, yb, K1; rep from * to last 2sts, K2.

  Change to yarn B.
- Rows 9+10: Knit.
- Rows 11+12: As rows 3+4 but in yarn C.
- Rows 13+14: Knit in yarn A.
- Rows 15+16: As rows 7+8 but in yarn B.
- Rows 17+18: Knit in yarn C.
- Rows 19+20: As rows 3+4 in yarn A.
- Rows 21+22: Knit in yarn B.
- Rows 23+24: As rows 7+8 in yarn C.

  These 24 rows make up one complete pattern; repeat until the scarf is the length you need ending on row 24.

  Knit 2 rows in yarn A.

  Cast off in yarn A, fasten off and weave in any loose ends.

  Add a fringe to the ends of the scarf to match your colours.

To add a fringe

Cut pieces of yarn double the length you want the fringe to be and fold them in half. With right side of work facing you insert a crochet hook down into your first stitch on the edge to be fringed, catch the loop of a piece of folded yarn and draw up through the stitch. Take the hook down into this loop and then catch the tails of yarn, pull them up through the loop and tighten. Continue to thread the fringe evenly along the edge. Yarn can be used double if you wish.

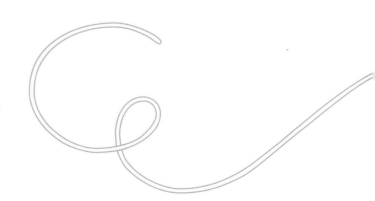

Baby helmet

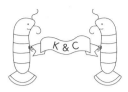

A funky baby hat incorporating simple stripes – be as bold and adventurous as you like with your colour scheme to make something really original. The garter stitch earflaps stay nice and flat (in contrast to stocking stitch which has a tendency to curl up) so that little ears are cosy and warm.

Measurements
To fit an average 3-6 month old

You will need
- Yarn: 1 x 50g (100m) DK in main colour (MC)
  1 x 50g (100m) DK in contrast colour (CC)
- Needles: 4mm
- Crochet hook: 4mm
- Stitch holder

Special note
sk2po – slip 1, knit 2 together, pass slipped stitch over, thus decreasing by 2 stitches.

Earflaps (make 2)
Cast on 1 stitch using CC.
- Row 1: Kfb. [2sts]
- Row 2: Kfb, K1. [3sts]
- Row 3: Kfb, K1, kfb. [5sts]
- Row 4: Kfb, K3, kfb. [7sts]
- Row 5: Kfb, K5, kfb. [9sts]
- Row 6: Kfb, K7, kfb. [11sts]
- Row 7: Kfb, K9, kfb. [13sts]
- Row 8: Kfb, K11, kfb. [15sts]
  Work 11 rows in garter stitch (every row knit).
- Next row: K6, k2tog, K7. [14sts]
  Leave these 14sts on a stitch holder.

Body of hat
Cast on 12sts using CC.
- With these stitches on the needle in your right hand now knit across 14sts on stitch holder for first earflap. Take needle with these 26sts back in your left hand and cast on another 24sts. Place needle with these 50sts back in your right hand and knit across 14sts at top of second earflap. Turn again and cast on a further 12sts. [76sts]
  Knit 5 rows.

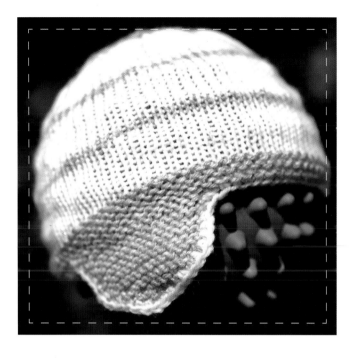

- Join in MC and work 10 rows st st – first row (rs) knit, second row (ws) purl.
- Join in CC and work 2 rows in st st.
  Repeat these 12 rows once more joining in MC and CC as required and then work 8 rows of st st in MC.

Begin shaping

- Next row: (rs) K24, k2togtbl, K24, k2tog, K24. [74sts]
- Next row: Purl.
  Join in CC.
- Next row: K4, sk2po, *K4, sk2po; rep from * another 8 times, K4. [54sts]
- Next row: Purl.
  Join in MC.
- Next row: Knit.
- Next row: Purl.
- Next row: K3, sk2po, *K2, sk2po; rep from * another 8 times, K3. [34sts]
- Next 3 rows: St st starting with a purl row.
- Next row: (rs) K2, (sk2po) 10 times, K2. [14sts]
- Next row: Purl.
  Thread yarn through remaining 14sts, pull up and fasten off securely. Weave in loose ends. Join back seam.

Edging

With MC and size 4mm crochet hook work one round of double crochet evenly round bottom edge starting at centre back and joining last dc to first dc with a sl st. Weave in ends.

For pets

Dog collar

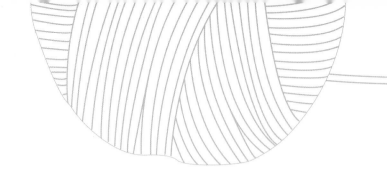

Everyone loves a crocheted gift and that includes your four-legged friends. Get your pet into the Christmas spirit with this collar in red and white, or make one for any occasion. Simply increase the number of stitches worked to get the perfect size for your dog.

Begin with a slip knot and yarn A; make 55 foundation chain.
• Row 1: Dc into 2nd ch from hook and each remaining ch. Turn. [54sts]
• Row 2: 2ch, tr into every dc across row. Turn. [54sts]
• Row 3: 2ch, dc in yarn A into each of next 3tr, join in yarn B (see page 29 and special note) and working into every tr across the row make 2dc in yarn B and 2dc in yarn A to the last 6sts (11 repeats), 2dc in yarn B, drop yarn B, 4dc in yarn A. Turn.
• Row 4: 2ch, 3dc in yarn A, pick up yarn B and place at the back of the work, 2dc in yarn B, *2dc in yarn A, 2dc in yarn B; rep from * to last 4sts, 4dc in yarn A. Turn.
Continue in yarn A as follows:
• Row 5: 2ch, tr into every st across row. Turn. [54sts]
• Row 6: 2ch, dc into every st across row. [54sts]
Fasten off and weave in any ends.
Using strong matching thread attach a snap fastener to right side of one end and wrong side of the other. Sew button onto right side over snap fastener.

Granny square dog coat

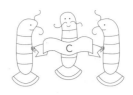

The crocheted granny square is so versatile: it can be used in blankets and throws, cushion covers, scarves, place mats and even dog coats! This one has been custom-made for a skinny whippet. Simply adapt the number of squares to fit a hound of any shape or size.

Measurements

The template for this coat is a 50cm x 40cm (20in x 16in) rectangle with 2 extra squares added at the head end for the neck fastening.

You will need

- Yarn: oddments of aran weight in a variety of colours
- Crochet hook: 5mm
- Buttons for the neck fastening

Special note

To work the granny square in a single colour do not break off your yarn at the end of each round. Join your round with a slip stitch into the 3rd of the 3 chains at the beginning of the round. Work 2 more slip stitches into the next 2 trebles and a slip stitch into the 3 chain space. In this way you move across to the next 3 chain space ready to begin the next round with 3 chains.

Tension

Each granny square in aran weight yarn measures 10cm x 10cm (4in x 4in). If you wish to make this project in DK yarn use a 4mm hook and work a square before you start; the size will give you an idea of how many you need to fit your dog. Similarly, the coat could be made in chunky weight (or DK worked double) with a 6mm hook.

The basic granny square

Instead of working in rows granny squares are crocheted in rounds. This basic granny square is made up of four rounds and you can introduce different colours whenever you want to. This pattern uses the technique of changing colour after each round but if you wish to stick to one colour for each square (as in this dog coat) see the special note.

- Foundation chain ring: Leaving a 15cm end make 6ch and join into a ring with a sl st into the first ch made.
- Rnd 1: 3ch, 2tr into ring, *3ch, 3tr into ring; rep from * twice more, 3ch, join with sl st to 3rd of initial 3ch. Break yarn and fasten off.
- Rnd 2: Join in next colour with a sl st by inserting hook with a slip knot on it into any 3ch space and drawing a loop

through, 3ch, (2tr, 3ch, 3tr) into same sp as sl st was worked, *1ch, (3tr, 3ch, 3tr) into next 3ch sp; rep from * twice more, 1ch, join with a sl st to 3rd of first 3ch. Break off yarn and fasten off.

- Rnd 3: Using next colour join in yarn with a sl st as in round 2, 3ch, (2tr, 3ch, 3tr) into same sp as sl st, *1ch, 3tr into next 1ch sp, 1ch, (3tr, 3ch, 3tr) into next 3ch sp; rep from * twice more, 1ch, 3tr into next 1ch sp, 1ch, join with a sl st to 3rd of first 3ch.
  Break off yarn and fasten off.
- Rnd 4: Using next colour join in yarn with a sl st as in rounds 2+3, 3ch, (2tr, 3ch, 3tr) into same sp as sl st, *(1ch, 3tr into next 1ch sp) twice, 1ch, (3tr, 3ch, 3tr) into next 3ch sp; rep from * twice more, (1ch, 3tr into next 1ch sp) twice, 1ch, join with sl st to 3rd of first 3ch.
  Fasten off.

To make up

The finished squares can be stitched together with a tapestry needle and strong matching yarn or joined with double crochet seams as follows:

Hold 2 squares with wrong sides together and match up the stitches as you go. Work a double crochet into the top of each stitch or chain space along the edge but insert the hook under the top 2 loops of the stitches of both squares at the same time.

Edging

Pick out one of the colours and double crochet 2 rounds all around the edge of the coat working one dc into every stitch and 3dc into every corner. The 2 extra squares fasten with buttons at the neck; the strap is a strip worked in double crochet for strength and is stitched onto the back of the coat with the addition of some strong Velcro patches for a secure fastening.

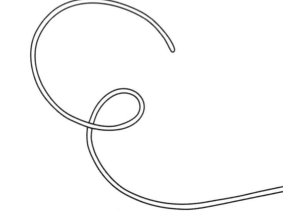

The difference knitting can make

Knitting is a fantastically rewarding and satisfying hobby but it can also be a way of bringing people together – a tool for inspiring people and a catalyst for communities to come together to make a real difference. Here are a few examples:

The founders of the knitting boutique Purlesque used knitting graffiti to engage with participants on the Art Valley project in Liverpool. The project used art as a way of tackling issues such as anti-social behaviour, isolation among older people and lack of confidence in young parents. Participants were taught finger knitting which is easy to learn and provides quick results. Creating graffiti intrigued even the most reluctant knitter.

Yarn Bomb the Castle was part of Lancashire County Council's 2012 arts development programme for young people. Local people who love knitting were encouraged to get involved to pass down their skills. The aim was to engage young people in a traditional craft, help them develop new skills and support future career opportunities. There were interactive, contemporary knitting workshops which culminated in Clitheroe Castle being accessorized in vibrant knitwear.

As part of Bournemouth's Big Green Fortnight and National Family Week in 2011 a knitted garden was installed and free family knitting workshops were run at Bournemouth Library. Over 1500 life size contributions were sent in including flowers, vegetables, a garden shed and tools, a washing line of knickers, foxes, hedgehogs, moles and molehills.

For Her

Arm & leg warmers

Leg warmers for your arms! Soft and snug during the winter months and brilliant for combatting cold steering wheels on chilly mornings. These arm warmers are knitted in a cashmerino yarn, a mix of cashmere, merino wool and silk but you can choose any yarn in DK weight. The four row pattern is a variation on basket rib and gives the arm warmers their stretchiness.

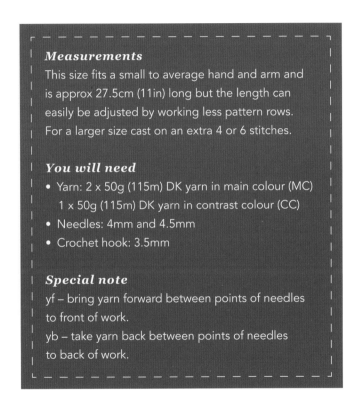

Measurements

This size fits a small to average hand and arm and is approx 27.5cm (11in) long but the length can easily be adjusted by working less pattern rows. For a larger size cast on an extra 4 or 6 stitches.

You will need

- Yarn: 2 x 50g (115m) DK yarn in main colour (MC)
  1 x 50g (115m) DK yarn in contrast colour (CC)
- Needles: 4mm and 4.5mm
- Crochet hook: 3.5mm

Special note

yf – bring yarn forward between points of needles to front of work.

yb – take yarn back between points of needles to back of work.

Cast on 41sts with 4mm needles in MC (this will be the lower edge of arm warmer).

- Row 1: (rs) Knit.
- Row 2: Purl.
- Row 3: K1, *sl1pw, K1; rep from * to end.
- Row 4: K1, *yf, sl1pw, yb, K1; rep from * to end.
  These 4 rows form the pattern. Work in stripes of 16 rows in MC followed by 4 rows in CC. After 60 rows change to size 4.5mm needles and work a further 72 rows keeping stripe sequence correct.
  Change to CC.
- Next row: *K1, P1; rep from * to last st, K1.
- Next row: *P1, K1; rep from * to last st, P1.
  Repeat the last 2 rows twice more.
  Cast off in rib (K1, P1). Fasten off and weave in loose ends.

To make up

Join side seam leaving 4cm open for thumb 4cm up from lower (cast-on) edge. Using 3.5mm crochet hook and CC double crochet around lower edge of arm warmer as follows: With rs facing join in yarn at the seam with a sl st, ch1 and dc evenly around the edge, joining to first ch with a sl st. Fasten off and weave in ends. Finish off the edge of the thumb opening in the same way.

Work second arm warmer the same as the first.

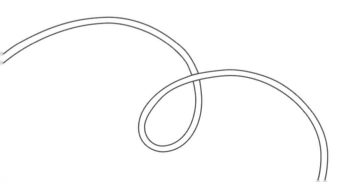

Little leg warmers

This stitch pattern can easily be adapted to make little leg warmers – as long as you cast on an odd number of stitches the size can be adjusted to fit any leg. Knit them in a single colour, use the same colour sequence as the arm warmers or introduce the stripes in any sequence you like. The following size should fit most two to three year olds.

You will need
- Yarn: 50g (115m) DK yarn plus oddments in a different colour if you want the striped ones
- Needles: 3mm, 3.25mm and 4mm

Using 3.25mm needles cast on 39 stitches.

Work 14 rows in K1, P1 rib – right side rows will start K1, P1 and wrong side rows will start P1, K1.

Change to 4mm needles and work the same 4 row pattern as for the arm warmers.

Kfb into the first and last stitches of rows 37+41 of the pattern. [43sts]

Change to 4.5mm needles and keeping the pattern correct on the extra stitches continue until you have worked 84 rows of pattern in all.

Change to 4mm needles and work 11 rows in K1, P1 rib. Cast off in rib.

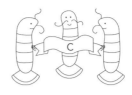

Granny square bag

Here the granny square is used to make a retro-looking and surprisingly strong bag. This design is made in DK cotton which produces a durable and firm fabric. Lighter or heavier yarns worked with smaller or larger hooks will give totally different effects: small hooks will give a tighter, more rigid bag while larger hooks will produce looser fabric with more drape.

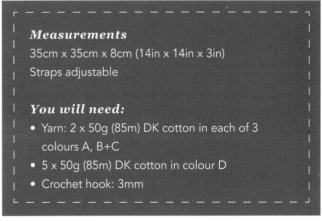

Measurements
35cm x 35cm x 8cm (14in x 14in x 3in)
Straps adjustable

You will need:
- Yarn: 2 x 50g (85m) DK cotton in each of 3 colours A, B+C
- 5 x 50g (85m) DK cotton in colour D
- Crochet hook: 3mm

The bag is made up of 18 granny squares, 9 each front and back worked in 3 or 4 different colours, edged and joined into 2 large squares in yarn D. The sides, base and straps of the bag are strips of double crochet which are then joined to the front and back with double crochet worked with wrong sides of the work together.

Granny square
- Foundation chain ring: Leaving a 15cm end make 6ch and join into a ring with a sl st into the first ch made.

- Rnd 1: Using same colour 3ch, 2tr into ring, *3ch, 3tr into ring; rep from * twice more, 3ch, join with sl st to 3rd of initial 3ch.
  Break off yarn and fasten off.
- Rnd 2: Join in next colour with a sl st by inserting hook (with a slip knot on it) into any 3ch space and drawing a loop through, 3ch, (2tr, 3ch, 3tr) into same sp as sl st was worked, *1ch, (3tr, 3ch, 3tr) into next 3ch sp; rep from * twice more, 1ch, join with a sl st to 3rd of first 3ch.
  Break off yarn and fasten off.
- Rnd 3: Using next colour join in yarn with a sl st as in round 2, 3ch, (2tr, 3ch, 3tr) into same sp as sl st, *1ch, 3tr into next ch sp, 1ch, (3tr, 3ch, 3tr) into next 3ch sp; rep from * twice more, 1ch, 3tr into next ch sp, 1ch, join with a sl st to 3rd of first 3ch.
  Break off yarn and fasten off.
- Rnd 4: Using next colour join in yarn with a sl st as in round 2, 3ch, (2tr, 3ch, 3tr) into same sp as sl st, *(1ch, 3tr into next ch sp) twice, 1ch, (3tr, 3ch, 3tr) into next 3ch sp; rep from * twice more, (1ch, 3tr into next 1ch sp) twice, 1ch, join with sl st to 3rd of first 3ch.
  Fasten off.
  Make 17 more squares working each round of each square in a different colour remembering that the edging of each one and the joining rounds will be in yarn D.

Edging

Edge the squares in yarn D with 2 rounds of dc as follows:
- Rnd 1: Join in yarn with a sl st into first ch of a 3ch group at a corner, 1ch, 1dc into same place as sl st was worked, 3dc into next ch (corner ch), 1dc into next ch, (1dc into each of next 3tr, 1dc into next ch) 3 times, 1dc into each of next 3tr, *1dc into first ch of next 3ch group, 3dc into next ch, 1dc into next ch, (1dc into each of next 3tr, 1dc into next ch) 3 times, 1dc into each of next 3tr; rep from * twice more, join with sl st into top of first dc of round.
- Rnd 2: 1ch, 1dc into same place as sl st worked, 1dc into each dc along the sides and 3dc into each corner dc (the centre dc of each 3dc group), join with a sl st to top of first dc. Fasten off.

To make up

For the front and back join squares in 3 rows of 3 by placing right sides together and either oversew or join with a row of dc into each stitch along edge. Work an outer border of 3 further rounds of dc in yarn D in exactly the same way as round 2 of edging. Fasten off and weave in any loose ends.

Sides and base

Make 3 strips of fabric in dc in a stripe sequence of 8 rows yarn D, 2 rows yarn A, 8 rows yarn D, 2 rows yarn B, 8 rows yarn D, 2 rows yarn C.
- Foundation row: Using yarn D make 15ch, dc into 2ch from hook and dc into each ch. Turn. [14sts]
- Row 1: 1ch (counts as first dc), dc into each st to end. Turn. Rep row 1 keeping stripe sequence correct until each strip is the required length for the bottom and two sides of the bag. Join front and back to the side panels by placing wrong sides together and working a dc into each st down the side seams. Then join in the base in the same way. The ridges produced at the seams will give a strong, firm finish to the bag.

Straps (make 2)

The length of the straps is up to you. Work strips of dc 8st wide (make 9ch and work into 2nd ch from hook) in stripes of whichever colours you have left or stick to a single colour if you prefer. When the strip is your required length fasten off and weave in any loose ends. Firmly oversew the ends of the straps to the top inside edges of the bag.

Headband

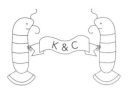

Halfway between earmuffs and a hat, you can dress them up or down and there is the added bonus that they don't mess up your hair. You can knit this to match your arm warmers or as a one-off. Cashmerino yarn is particularly soft but any DK will work.

Measurements

The headband is quite stretchy so should fit an average size adult head.

You will need

- Yarn: 1 x 50g (115m) DK in main colour (MC)
- Small amount of DK in contrast colour (CC) to edge the headband and decorate with a flower if you wish
- Needles: 4mm
- Crochet hook: 3.5mm and 4mm

Cast on 21sts using MC.

- Row 1: Knit.
- Row 2: Purl.
- Row 3: K1, *sl1pw, K1; rep from * to end.
- Row 4: K1, *yf, sl1pw, yb, K1; rep from * to end.
  These 4 rows form the pattern.
  Work rows 1-4 49 times or until your band is long enough to fit snugly around your head.
  Cast off.
  Fasten off and weave in loose ends.

To make up

Fold headband in two with right sides together and oversew cast-on and cast-off edges.

Using 3.5mm crochet hook and with right side facing join in CC at edge of back seam with a sl st.

- Rnd 1: Make 1 chain then double crochet evenly around outer edge of headband. At end of round join to first ch with sl st.
- Rnd 2: 1ch then dc into each st to end, sl st into first ch. Fasten off and weave in loose ends.
  Work around the other side of the headband in CC in exactly the same way.

Crochet flower

Using 4mm crochet hook and CC make 4ch; join with sl st to first ch to form a ring.

- Rnd 1: (3ch, dc in ring) 4 times, 3ch, sl st to base of first 3ch.
- Rnd 2: (petal) Work (dc, 1ch, 3tr, 1ch, dc) in each 3ch space, sl st to first ch at beg of first petal.
- Rnd 3: Push the next petal forward so that you can work behind and sl st into back of first dc made in previous rnd, *4ch, dc into back of work between next 2 petals. Rep from * 3 more times, 4ch, sl st to first ch of rnd 3 to join.
- Rnd 4: (petal) Work (dc, htr, tr, 2dtr, ch, 2dtr, tr, htr, dc) in each 4ch sp, sl st to first dc to join.
  Fasten off and weave in ends. Attach flower securely to headband; the easiest way to do this is with matching sewing thread and a tapestry needle, working a couple of rounds of small stitches around the centre of the flower.

Crochet Belt

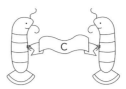

There's plenty of scope for experimentation here. This striking design can be worked in different weight yarns depending on what you want to create. Use anything from an aran weight yarn for a chunky belt to a fine, laceweight silk mix or 4ply cotton for a great looking, original necklace or bracelet.

You will need
- Yarn: Any yarn you choose can be crocheted but fluffy ones tend to be more difficult to work with as the stitch definition is less obvious

Special note
Tension and measurements in this project depend entirely on the yarn and effect selected.

Choose a hook to suit your chosen yarn; a fine hook will produce a firm, tight fabric while a thicker one will give your finished item more drape and a softer look. It might be worth experimenting with different hooks and oddments of yarn before you decide which you prefer.

- Foundation row: Ch6, 1htr in 3rd ch from hook (ring made), *(ch8, 1htr in 3rd ch from hook); rep from * until you have enough rings to make your belt, ch 3.
- Row 1: Miss 3ch, *work (4tr, ch1, 4tr) in next ring, miss 2ch, sl st in next ch, miss 2ch; rep from * across to last ch, sl st in last ch.
- Turn to work across opposite side of foundation row, miss 2ch; rep from * (row 1) across, join with sl st in last ch of foundation row.
  Fasten off and weave in loose ends.

The belt can be finished off by adding a popper to the last ring at each end, you can add a button and use the first ring as a buttonhole (remembering to add an extra ring in this case for the overlap) or you can add a fringe and decorate with some beads.

Fingerless mittens

Most gloves are knitted on four needles which can be tricky, so why not start by trying this fingerless version knitted on two needles? A self-patterning yarn will give a Fair Isle effect or try two or three stripes for a more vibrant look. The rib at the wrist and at the cast-off edge work really well in a contrasting colour to the body of the mitten.

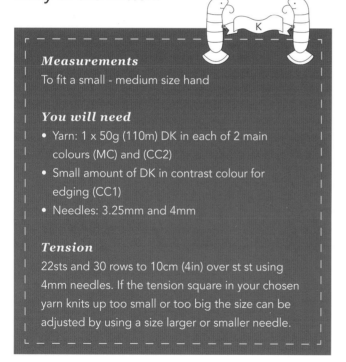

Measurements
To fit a small - medium size hand

You will need
- Yarn: 1 x 50g (110m) DK in each of 2 main colours (MC) and (CC2)
- Small amount of DK in contrast colour for edging (CC1)
- Needles: 3.25mm and 4mm

Tension
22sts and 30 rows to 10cm (4in) over st st using 4mm needles. If the tension square in your chosen yarn knits up too small or too big the size can be adjusted by using a size larger or smaller needle.

Right hand mitten
Using 3.25mm needles cast on 44sts in CC1.
- Row 1: (ws) *K1, P1; rep from * to end.
- Row 2: (rs) Join in CC2 and knit to end.
- Rows 3-17: In CC2 work in K1, P1 rib.
- Row 18: (rs) Join in CC1 and knit.
- Row 19: (ws) In CC1 *K1, P1; rep from * to end.
  Change to 4mm needles.
- Row 20: Join in MC, K14, k2tog, K12, k2tog, K14. [42sts]
  Work 7 more rows in st st beginning with a purl row.
- Row 28: K21, m1, K3, m1, K to end. [44sts]
- Row 29 and every odd row: Purl.
- Row 30: K21, m1, K5, m1, K to end. [46sts]
- Row 32: K21, m1, K7, m1, K to end. [48sts]
- Row 34: K21, m1, K9, m1, K to end. [50sts]
- Row 36: K21, m1, K11, m1, K to end. [52sts]
- Row 38: K21, m1, K13, m1, K to end. [54sts]
- Row 39: Purl.

Divide for thumb
- Next row: K36, turn.
- Next row: P15, turn.
  Work 4 rows of st st on these 15sts only, starting with a knit row.
- Join in CC1 and work 2 rows st st.
  Cast off in CC1.
- With rs facing rejoin MC to remaining 18sts at base of thumb and knit to end. [39sts]
- Next row: Purl.
  Work 4 more rows st st ending with ws row.
- Join in CC1 and knit to end.
- Next row: Purl.
  Change to 3.25mm needles and CC2.
- Next row: (rs) Knit.
  Work 5 rows in K1, P1 rib starting with P1.

- Join in CC1 and knit to end.
  Cast off in rib in CC1.
  Fasten off and weave in loose ends.

Left hand mitten

Repeat as for right hand mitten until row 27.

- Row 28: K18, m1, K3, m1, K to end. [44sts]
  Work increase rows 30, 32, 34, 36 and 38 as for the other mitten but knit 18sts before first increase. [54sts]
- Row 39: Purl.

Divide for thumb

- Next row: Knit 33, turn.
- Next row: Purl 15, turn.

Work 4 rows st st on these 15sts only, starting with a knit row.

- Join in CC1 and work 2 rows st st.
  Cast off in CC1.
- With rs facing rejoin MC to rem 21sts at base of thumb and knit to end. [39sts]
- Next row: Purl.
  Work 4 more rows st st ending with a ws row.
- Join in CC1 and knit to end.
- Next row: Purl.
  Change to 3.25mm needles and CC2.
  Complete mitten as for right hand.

To make up

With right sides together sew up side and thumb seams.

Knitting as therapy

Knitting isn't a miracle cure, but healthcare professionals are starting to recognise the therapeutic benefits and the potential of knitting as an accessible and cheap healthcare tool.

Research shows that the bilateral rhythmic movements of knitting have an effect on the brain and nervous system. It's an excellent method of stress management, can help people quit smoking or binge eating, helps people with depression and can help manage illness and pain.

And the evidence really does stack up.

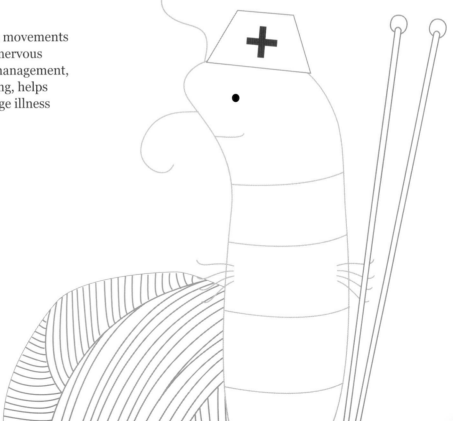

Here's how it works.

There are proven psychological and social benefits to knitting. Knitting raises self-esteem and confidence. Learning a new skill and being in control make you feel good and the concentration needed for knitting can distract your mind, giving it a break from the daily grind. Loneliness and isolation have a big impact on well-being and knitting can be a link for people to join a supportive community, whether through online forums or face-to-face knitting groups.

Moving on to the science bit – the bilateral rhythmic movements of knitting have a calming effect on the brain and nervous system that encourages deep relaxation. Relaxation lowers levels of stress hormones that intensify issues such as pain, depression and anxiety.

The repetitive nature of movements is important too. They enhance the release of the hormone serotonin which raises mood and acts as a pain killer. The automatic nature of movements lodges in the subconscious and can help push out negative thought processes that get stuck there too. Evidence from patients suggests that knitting can also reduce the frequency of flashbacks after a traumatic event.

Neurologically, it is known that new brain cells can be born and opened up, no matter what age you are. But if you don't use your brain connections they will be broken and pathways lost. It's also known that occupied people feel less pain than unoccupied people. So why do we see millions of older people sitting around in hospitals and care homes doing nothing? Knitting can help to change this, it can help manage pain, offer a supportive community and be a fun and creative outlet for anyone of any age.

Colour and texture have an impact too and can raise mood significantly. If something feels luxurious and soft to touch it makes us feel good. If a yarn is a beautiful colour but is rough and hard to knit, surveys have shown that it lessens the therapeutic effect.

Betsan Corkin, founder of Stitchlinks (an organisation which researches the therapeutic benefits of knitting) has set up knitting groups for pain management and is building up evidence to support knitting being introduced into mainstream healthcare. Other pain clinics are following her lead.

You can find out more at www.stitchlinks.com

FOR HIM

Tie

They cost a fortune on the High Street but you can make your own for a fraction of the price and a whole lot more satisfaction. Use any self-patterning sock wool to make this unique and great looking tie. Knitted entirely in garter stitch this is an excellent beginner's project. The yarn is used double throughout so you will need two balls of yarn.

Measurements
135cm (52in)

You will need
- Yarn: 2 x 50g (210m) 4ply or sock wool
- Needles: 3mm

Special note
Work with 2 strands of yarn together. Increase by knitting into front and back of stitch (kfb).

Cast on 1 stitch.

Inc into first st of every row until you have 23sts on your needle (22 rows).

For the remainder of your work slip the first stitch of every row.

- Row 23: (rs) K11, k2tog, K10. [22sts]
  Knit 7 rows.
- Row 31: K10, k2tog, K10. [21sts]
  Knit 7 rows.
- Row 39: K9, k2tog, K10. [20sts]
  Knit 7 rows.
- Row 47: K9, k2tog, K9. [19sts]
  Knit 7 rows.
- Row 55: K9, k2tog, K8. [18sts]
  Knit 11 rows.
- Row 67: K8, k2tog, K8. [17sts]
  Knit 13 rows.
- Row 81: K8, k2tog, K7. [16sts]
  Knit 15 rows.
- Row 97: K7, k2tog, K7. [15sts]
  Knit 39 rows.
- Row 137: K6, k2tog, K7. [14sts]
  Knit 39 rows.

- Row 177: K6, k2tog, K6. [13sts]
  Knit 15 rows.
- Row 193: K6, k2tog, K5. [12sts]
  Knit 15 rows.
- Row 209: K5, k2tog, K5. [11sts]
  Knit 15 rows.
- Row 225: K4, k2tog, K5. [10sts]
  Knit 35 rows.
- Row 261: K4, k2tog, K4. [9sts]
  Knit 45 rows.
- Row 307: K4, k2tog, K3. [8sts]
  Knit 45 rows.
- Row 353: K3, k2tog, K3. [7sts]
  Knit until tie measures 96cm or desired length – an odd number of rows so that right side is facing for next row.
- Next row: K3, kfb, K3. [8sts]
  Knit 45 rows.
- Next row: K4, kfb, K3. [9sts]
  Continue to work on these 9sts until tie measures 135cm or desired length from beginning.
  Next 7 rows: Sl1, k2tog, knit to end. [2sts]
- Next row: K2tog.
  Fasten off and weave in any loose ends.

Knitting for charity

Knitting and crocheting for charity is turning into a big thing. It's easy to get involved in and there is great scope for creativity, meeting new people and making a positive difference. You could knit some bits and bobs for a stall at a school fête or craft fair, you could support a charity art installation, you could get involved in one of the many global knitting projects or you could start up your own.

There have been some great projects over recent years which have really captured people's imaginations, including knitting toy donkeys to sell at The Donkey Sanctuary in Devon and making tiny hats for bottles of Innocent smoothies to raise money for Help the Aged and Age Concern. They are fun, quick projects where you really feel that you are giving something back.

For ideas of current charity knitting projects have a look at www.knittingforcharity.org Other ongoing projects are:

www.angelbear.org.uk who knit and crochet bears for children in crisis across the globe, supplying refuges, hospices, orphanages, children's homes and hospitals.

Bonnie Babies www.bonniebabies.co.uk send out tiny hats, blankets, clothing and burial outfits to premature babies and their families across UK hospitals.

The Knit-a-Square project www.knit-a-square.com where you can knit or crochet a square to be sewn into a blanket to keep AIDS orphans warm in South Africa.

P/hop – pennies per hour of pleasure raises money for the Médecins Sans Frontières medical aid organisation. Designers donate their knitting patterns and the idea is that you then make a donation based on how many hours of pleasure you will get from knitting your p/hop pattern www.p-hop.co.uk

Golf
club
cover

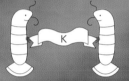

FOr
Sport

You don't find them like this in the shops – like a tea cosy for a golf club and a perfect gift for any golfer. This pineapple-like golf club cover knitted in a combination of bramble and rib stitches and decorated with a tassel or pompom can be made using either aran or chunky weight yarn.

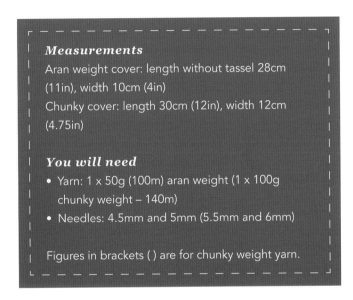

Measurements

Aran weight cover: length without tassel 28cm (11in), width 10cm (4in)

Chunky cover: length 30cm (12in), width 12cm (4.75in)

You will need

- Yarn: 1 x 50g (100m) aran weight (1 x 100g chunky weight – 140m)
- Needles: 4.5mm and 5mm (5.5mm and 6mm)

Figures in brackets ( ) are for chunky weight yarn.

Cast on 56(44) sts with 5(6)mm needles and work 24(14) rows in K2, P2 rib.

Change to 4.5(5.5)mm needles.

- Next row: *K2tog, p2tog; rep from * to end. [28(22) sts]
  Work 6 rows in K1, P1 rib.
- Next row: *Inc into next st by knitting into front and back of stitch (kfb); rep from * to end. [56(44) sts]
  Now work in pattern as follows:
- Row 1: (rs) Purl.
- Row 2: *(K1, P1, K1) into next st, p3tog; rep from * to end.
- Row 3: Purl.
- Row 4: *P3tog, (K1, P1, K1) into next st; rep from * to end.
  These 4 rows form the bramble stitch pattern.

For aran weight continue in pattern until work measures 26cm (10.25in), if using chunky yarn repeat these 4 rows 5 more times ending with a wrong side row.

Shape top

- Row 1: *P2tog, P1; rep from * to last 2sts, p2tog. [37(29) sts]
- Row 2: Knit.
- Row 3: P1, *p2tog; rep from * to end. [19(15) sts]
- Row 4: Knit.
  Break yarn, thread through remaining stitches and fasten off securely.

To make up

Do not press as this will flatten the texture of the bramble stitch pattern. Join side seam. Finish off with a tassel or a pompom.

Tassel

- You will need a piece of stiff cardboard the length you want the tassel to be. Wrap the yarn around the cardboard lengthways approximately 20 times. Now thread a piece of yarn under all the strands at one end of the cardboard and tie round them to secure. Cut the ends of yarn at the bottom and remove the card.
- Take another piece of yarn and wrap it tightly around the tassel about 2cm from the top. Knot tightly and pull the ends to the inside of the tassel with your needle.

FOR THE HOME

Tea cosy

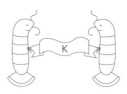

Super practical but also stylish-looking and straightforward to make – there's something about tea cosies. This two-coloured slip stitch design is easier than it looks and you can decorate it by adding knitted or crocheted flowers to the top. Threading some ribbon or an i-cord through the holes to gather the top is simple and effective.

Knit 2 pieces

Cast on 48sts with 4mm needles in MC.

Work 2.5cm in garter stitch (every row knit).

- Next row: K9, kfb, K9, kfb, K8, kfb, K9, kfb, K9. [52sts]
  Change to 4.5mm needles.
  Work in pattern as follows:

- Row 1: (rs) In MC knit.
- Row 2: (ws) In MC knit.
- Row 3: In CC K1, *sl2pw, K2; rep from * to last 3 sts, sl2pw, K1.
- Row 4: In CC K1, yf *sl2pw, P2; rep from * to last 3 sts, sl2pw, yb, K1.
  Repeat these 4 rows 15 times carrying yarns up the side of your work as you go.
  Change to size 4mm needles and continue in MC.
  Knit 2 rows.
- Next row: (eyelet row) K3, (k2tog, yo, K3) 9 times, k2tog, yo, K2.
- Next row: Purl.
  Knit 8 rows.
  Change to CC.
  Knit 2 rows.
  Cast off in CC. Fasten off and weave in any loose ends.

To make up

Join the side seams leaving openings at either side to fit your teapot handle and spout. Make a 65cm i-cord in CC. Thread through eyelets, gather top and tie in a bow or alternatively thread with contrasting ribbon and add any decorations to the top.

I-cord

You will need two 4mm double pointed needles. Cast on 3 stitches and knit 1 row. Without turning your needle slide the stitches to the right hand end. Pull the yarn tightly across the back and knit the stitches again. Continue to slide the stitches to the other end of the needle after each row and knit them again with the yarn pulled tight. After a few rows the knitting will form a tube. Continue until the cord is the length you need, cut the yarn, thread it down through the cord to secure and fasten off.

Cushion cover

This multi-coloured cushion cover is an excellent project for using up odd balls of different coloured DK yarns which you may have in your stash, or go for any colour scheme you fancy. Another option is to try this pattern in a single colour as the crochet stitch produces an interesting texture.

The stitch pattern is worked in multiples of 8+6 so if a cushion cover doesn't appeal you could adapt this pattern for a blanket or throw of any size using any weight yarn from DK to chunky. Remember to increase your hook size if you are using a thicker yarn – try 5.5/6mm for aran and 6.5/7mm for chunky or you can experiment with a tension square.

Measurements

Fits a 40cm (16in) square cushion pad

You will need

- Yarn: 3 x 50g (100m) DK in green (A)
  2 x 50g (100m) DK in brown (B)
  1 x 50g (100m) DK in each of the following colours: orange (C), yellow (D), red (E), cream (F) and terracotta (G)
- Crochet hook: 4.5mm
- 5 large buttons

Tension

16sts and 16 rows = 10cm (4in) over pattern using a 100% wool DK. If you are using a different DK yarn you may need to change your hook size to get these measurements.

Special note

Long treble crochet (lng tr) – yo 3 times, insert hook in st indicated, yo, draw loop up to height of working row, (yo, draw through 2 loops on hook) 3 times.

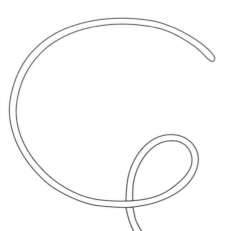

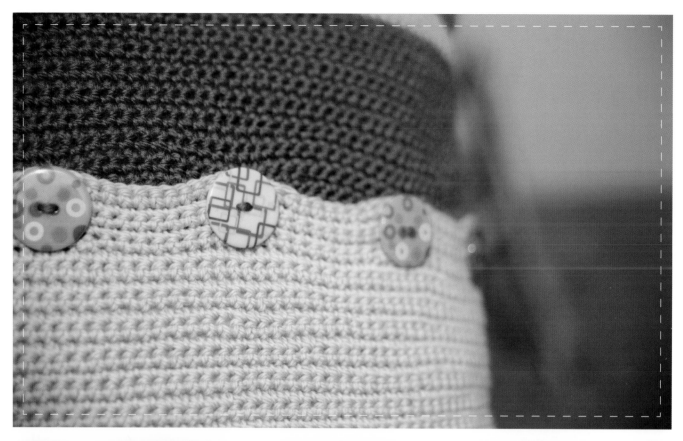

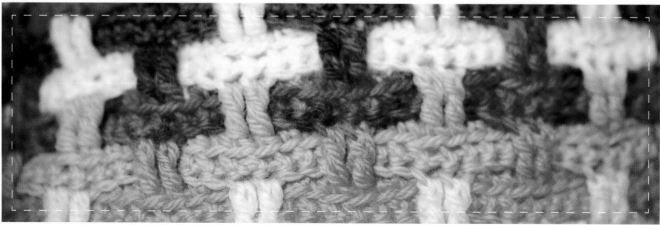

Front of cushion

With yarn D and 4.5mm hook make 63ch foundation row.

- Row 1: (rs) Dc into 2nd ch from hook, dc into each rem ch across. Turn. [62sts]
- Row 2: (ws) 1ch (does not count as first st), working into front loops only dc into each of 62dc across row, joining in yarn E at last st (see page 29). Turn.
- Row 3: 1ch, dc in back loop of same st, working in back loops only dc into each rem dc across row. Turn.
- Row 4: As row 2 but join in yarn B at last dc. Turn.
- Row 5: 1ch, dc into back loop of first 2sts, lng tr in front lp of next 2 corresponding dc 3 rows below, *skipping 2dc of row 4 behind 2lng tr just made, dc into back lp of each of next 6dc, lng tr into front lp of next 2 corresponding dc 3 rows below; rep from * to last 2dc, dc into back lp of last 2dc. Turn.
- Row 6: As row 2 but join in yarn F at last dc. Turn.
- Row 7: 1ch, dc into back lp of first 6sts, *lng tr in front lp of next 2 corresponding sts 3 rows below, skip 2dc from row 6 behind 2lng tr just made, dc into back lp of next 6dc; rep from * to end. Turn.
- Row 8: As row 2 but join in yarn G at last dc. Turn.
- Row 9+10: As rows 5+6 but join in yarn A at last dc. Turn.
- Row 11+12: As rows 7+8 but join in yarn C at last dc. Turn.
- Row 13+14: As rows 5+6 but join in yarn F at last dc. Turn.
Repeat rows 5–8 in this way keeping to the stripe sequence D, E, B, F, G, A, C, F until 34 stripes have been worked in all (68 rows). Fasten off and weave in all the ends.

Back of cushion cover (worked in 2 sections)
Lower back flap

Using yarn A and with wrong side of work facing you work 60dc evenly into foundation row of the cushion cover front. Turn.

- Row 1: 1ch (counts as first st on every row), dc into rem 59sts across row. Turn. [60sts]
Repeat this row 36 times or until flap measures half the depth of the front.
- Buttonhole row: 1ch, 1dc into each of next 4dc, (2ch, miss 2dc, 1dc into each of next 10dc) 4 times, 2ch, miss 2dc, 1dc into each of next 5dc (5 buttonholes made). Turn.
- Next row: 2ch, 1dc into each of next 4dc, (2dc into 2ch sp, 1dc into each of next 10dc) 4 times, 2dc into 2ch sp, 1dc into each of next 5dc. Turn.
Repeat row 1 three times.
Fasten off.
This section of the back should measure just over half the depth of the front of your cushion cover.

Upper back flap

Using yarn B and 4.5mm hook and with wrong side of work facing you work 60dc into last row of dc at top front of cushion cover. Turn.

- Row 1: 1ch, (counts as first st on every row), dc into rem 59dc across row. [60sts]
Repeat row 1 another 13 times changing to yarn C on last dc. Turn.
- Work 6 rows as row 1 in yarn C. Rejoin yarn B on last dc. Turn.
- Work 24 rows as row 1 in yarn B.
Fasten off.

To make up

Fold over back flaps and with wrong sides together use yarn G to join side seams with double crochet leaving the 6 rows of the buttonhole border on the lower back flap unsewn to overlap at centre back. Work another row of dc in yarn G around the whole cushion cover excluding buttonhole border. Sew buttons onto edge of upper back flap to match buttonholes.

Yarns used for the projects

The Woolly Prawn
- Stylecraft Life Aran – 100g, 75% acrylic, 25% wool, 198m
- Wendy Peter Pan DK – 50g, 55% nylon, 45% acrylic, 170m

Bunting
- Patons Diploma Gold DK – 50g, 55% wool, 25% acrylic, 20% nylon, 120m

Mix and match blanket
- Debbie Bliss Cashmerino DK – 50g, 55% merino wool, 33% microfibre, 12% cashmere, 110m
- Sublime (Baby) Cashmere Merino Silk DK – 50g, 75% merino wool, 20% silk, 5% cashmere, 116m

Baby helmet
- Rico Classic Baby DK – 50g, 50% acrylic, 50% polyamide, 165m

Child's scarf
- Lang Zoom – 50g, 60% wool, 30% cotton, 10% nylon, 160m

Dog collar
- Patons Diploma Gold DK – 50g, 55% wool, 25% acrylic, 20% nylon, 120m

Granny square dog coat
- Robin Bonny Babe Aran – 100g, 100% acrylic, 200m
- Wendy Aran with Wool – 100g, 75% acrylic, 25% wool, 200m
- Oddments of other coloured yarns

Arm warmers and leg warmers
- Debbie Bliss Cashmerino DK – 50g, 55% merino wool, 33% microfibre, 12% cashmere, 110m
- Sublime (Baby) Cashmere Merino Silk DK – 50g, 75% merino wool, 20% silk, 5% cashmere, 116m

Headband
- Debbie Bliss Cashmerino DK – 50g, 55% merino wool, 33% microfibre, 12% cashmere, 110m

Crochet belt
- Chunky belt: aran 100% wool
- Fine belt: hand-dyed sock wool

Fingerless mittens
- Wendy Peter Pan DK – 50g, 55% nylon, 45% acrylic, 170m

Granny square bag
- Rowan Handknit Cotton – 50g, 100% cotton, 85m

Tie
- Regia 4ply sock wool – 50g, 75% wool, 25% polyamide, 210m

Golf club cover
- Aran weight: Rowan Lima – 50g, 84% baby alpaca, 8% merino wool, 8% nylon, 100m
- Chunky weight: Wendy Mode Chunky – 100g, 50% merino wool, 50% acrylic, 100m

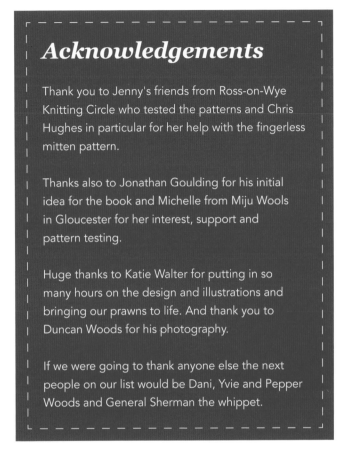

Acknowledgements

Thank you to Jenny's friends from Ross-on-Wye Knitting Circle who tested the patterns and Chris Hughes in particular for her help with the fingerless mitten pattern.

Thanks also to Jonathan Goulding for his initial idea for the book and Michelle from Miju Wools in Gloucester for her interest, support and pattern testing.

Huge thanks to Katie Walter for putting in so many hours on the design and illustrations and bringing our prawns to life. And thank you to Duncan Woods for his photography.

If we were going to thank anyone else the next people on our list would be Dani, Yvie and Pepper Woods and General Sherman the whippet.

Tea cosy
- King Cole Merino Blend DK – 50g, 100% wool, 112m

Cushion cover
- Patons Fairytale Colour 4 Me – 50g, 100% wool, 90m

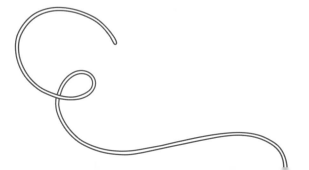